ACE!

By Mark Woods and Ruth Owen

Gareth Stevens
Publishing

ACE!

By Mark Woods and Ruth Owen

Gareth Stevens
Publishing

Please visit our Web site, www.garethstevens.com. For a free color catalog of all our high-quality books, call toll free 1-800-542-2595 or fax 1-877-542-2596.

Library of Congress Cataloging-in-Publication Data

Woods, Mark.
Ace! : tennis facts and stats / Mark Woods and Ruth Owen.
  p. cm. — (Top math)
ISBN 978-1-4339-4986-9 (library binding)
1. Tennis—Juvenile literature. 2. Tennis—Mathematics—Juvenile literature. I. Owen, Ruth, 1967- II. Title.
GV996.5.W66 2011
796.342—dc22

                    2010025704

Published in 2011 by
Gareth Stevens Publishing
111 East 14th Street, Suite 349
New York, NY 10003

© Ruby Tuesday Books Limited 2010

Developed & Created by Ruby Tuesday Books Ltd

Project Director – Ruth Owen
Designer – Alix Wood
Editor – Ben Hubbard
Consultants – Sally Smith, Hilary Koll, and Steve Mills

Images: Getty 9 (Getty Images Sport), 12 (Hamish Blair), 14 left (AFP Images), 15 (Hulton Archive), 16 right, 17 (Focus on Sport), 18 left (Chris Wilkins), 19 (Bob Thomas), 22 top (Stephen Dunn), 22 bottom (Steve Powell), 24 (Lluis Gene). Public domain 14 right. Shutterstock front cover, title page, 6–7 all, 8, 10, 13, 20, 21 all, 26, 27, 28, 29. Wikipedia (public domain) 16 left, 18 right, 23.

Printed in the United States of America

CPSIA compliance information: Batch #CW11GS: For further information contact Gareth Stevens, New York, New York at 1-800-542-2595.

CONTENTS

POINTS MEAN CHAMPIONS 6

RECORD BREAKERS 8

GAME, SET, AND MATCH 10

GRAND SLAMS 12

BLAST FROM THE PAST – THE MEN 14

BLAST FROM THE PAST – THE WOMEN 16

GREATEST FEMALE PLAYERS 18

ROGER FEDERER – THE BEST EVER? 20

GREATEST MALE PLAYERS 22

THE DAVIS CUP AND FED CUP 24

THE WILLIAMS SISTERS 26

NADAL VS MURRAY 28

ANSWERS 30

GLOSSARY 31

INDEX 32

POINTS MEAN CHAMPIONS

Numbers are everywhere in tennis. Aces, game points, set points, and match points. To become a champion, every shot must count and the points have to add up!

ACE

Each point in tennis begins with a serve – one player hitting the ball over the net. If your serve goes into an area called the service box in your opponent's half of the court and he or she can't return the serve (hit the ball back), it's called an ace.

Becoming a champion tennis player takes practice. It's the same with numbers. When you practice your math skills, you improve your math fitness.

Venus Williams

Serena Williams

and Serena Williams are experts at making every shot count. By July 2010, Serena had won 13 Grand Slams. Venus had won seven. The sisters had also won 11 Grand Slam doubles titles together.

Tennis is played on four kinds of surface – hard court (often cement), grass, carpet (indoors), and clay. The ball will bounce at different heights on each surface. The players will also move in different ways because of the amount of grip beneath their feet. It almost means four different types of tennis!

GRAND SLAM

A Grand Slam is when a player wins one of the four biggest tennis tournaments. The Grand Slams are the Australian Open, the French Open, Wimbledon, and the US Open.

Let's get started!

RECORD BREAKERS

Let's look at some of the records that have made tennis a smash over the years.

Andy Roddick serves.

FASTEST SERVE

American tennis player Andy Roddick holds the record for the fastest serve. During a game in 2004, Andy's serve was measured at 155 mph.

LONGEST MATCH

The longest match ever took place between John Isner and Nicolas Mahut at Wimbledon in 2010. John Isner won the match after an incredible 11 hours and five minutes.

SHORTEST GRAND SLAM FINAL

The shortest Grand Slam final happened at the French Open in 1988. Steffi Graf beat Natasha Zvereva in just 32 minutes. The score was 6–0, 6–0.

ALL-TIME TOP EARNERS

Player	Prize money in dollars
Roger Federer	$50.8 million
Pete Sampras	$43.3 million
Andre Agassi	$31.1 million
Rafael Nadal	$25.2 million
Boris Becker	$25.1 million

(Statistics up to September 2009)

CONSECUTIVE WINS

Sometimes players win matches consecutively – one after another with no losses.

	Consecutive matches won	Year
Martina Navratilova	74	1984
Steffi Graf	66	1989–90
Martina Navratilova	58	1986–87

Martina Navratilova in action in 1987.

RECORD BREAKERS QUIZ

Try these quiz questions about tennis record breakers.

1) The longest-ever match lasted **11 hours 5 minutes**. How long is that in minutes?

2) How long is a tennis match if it starts at **2:00 pm** and finishes at **5:35 pm**? Give your answer in hours and minutes.

3) What is the difference in prize money earnings between top earner Roger Federer and each of the other four players in the list?

4) Steffi Graf won the shortest ever match in 32 minutes. Steffi played and won 12 games to win the match. If 8 of the 32 minutes were spent changing ends and resting, what was the average length of each of the 12 games?

5) Look at the **Consecutive Wins** list. Use the numbers of matches won to make as many different calculations as you can in five minutes. Here's one to get you started: **74 + 66 – 58 = 82**

GAME, SET, AND MATCH

The aim of tennis is to hit the ball over the net into your opponent's half of the court so that your opponent is unable to hit it back. If you can do this, you win the point. If you hit the ball into the net or outside the lines of the playing area, your opponent wins the point.

This is the outside line for doubles.

This is the outside line for singles.

IN AND OUT

IN – A ball inside or on the line.
OUT – A ball outside the line.

HOW TO SCORE IN TENNIS

Tennis matches are played as the best of three or five sets. To win a set, a player must be the first to win six games.

HOW TO WIN A GAME – THE BASICS

A player needs four points to win a game. The four points are counted as **15, 30, 40,** then **game**.

If the score reaches **40–40**, one player must score two more points to win the game.

The first point a player scores at this stage is called **advantage (AD)**.

If the same player wins the next point, that player wins the game.

If the player loses the point, the score returns to **40–40** and the process begins again.

HOW TO WIN A SET – THE BASICS

The first player to win six games wins the set. However, if the score reaches **5–5**, one player must go two games ahead to win the set, for example, **7–5**.

If the players get to **6–6**, they can play a 13th game called a tiebreaker.

SCORING QUIZ

Read about how to score in tennis, then see if you could score a championship match!

Look at the scores below.

	Score A	Score B	Score C
Murray	15	30	40
Federer	15	15	30

1) How many times has each player scored? For example, in the Score A column each player has scored once.

2) Look at Score C. Who is closer to winning the game?

Now look at this match scoreboard. The players are playing set five.

PREVIOUS SETS					SET 5 Games
6	5	4	6	Roddick	5
3	7	6	2	Federer	3

3) How many games did Federer win in the first four sets? Which sets did he win?

4) If Roddick wins the next game, will he win the match?

5) To win a set, a player must win at least six games. If a match is the best of five sets, what is the lowest number of games a player could win to take the match?

GRAND SLAMS

The four biggest tournaments in tennis are known as the "Grand Slams." Each tournament is held over two weeks. The best men, women, and juniors in the world take part in singles and doubles competitions.

The Wimbledon men's winner receives a trophy that says, "The All England Lawn Tennis Club Single Handed Champion of the World." Here, Rafael Nadal lifts the Wimbledon trophy in 2010.

AUSTRALIAN OPEN

Tournament began: 1905
Location: Melbourne, Australia
Surface: Hard courts
When held: January

FRENCH OPEN

Tournament began: 1891
Location: Paris, France
Surface: Clay
When held: May/June

WIMBLEDON

Tournament began: 1877
Location: London, UK
Surface: Grass
When held: June/July

US OPEN

Tournament began: 1881
Location: New York City, NY
Surface: Hard courts
When held: August/September

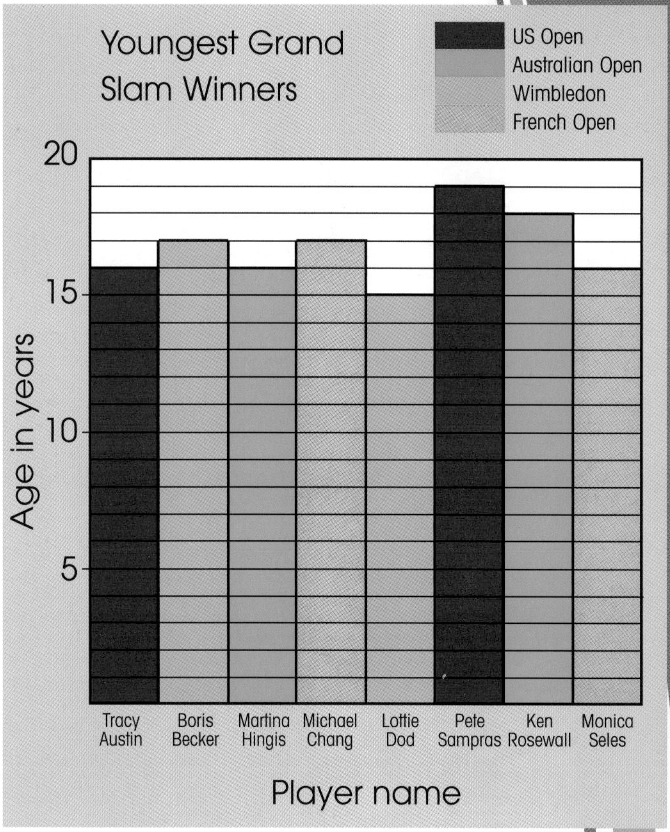

GRAND SLAM QUIZ

Youngest Grand Slam Winners

Legend:
- US Open
- Australian Open
- Wimbledon
- French Open

Bar chart — Age in years (vertical axis, 0 to 20) vs Player name (horizontal axis):
- Tracy Austin
- Boris Becker
- Martina Hingis
- Michael Chang
- Lottie Dod
- Pete Sampras
- Ken Rosewall
- Monica Seles

Around 52,000 tennis balls are used at Wimbledon. Each ball is hand tested for bounce and weight.

Try these Grand Slam quiz questions.

1) Look at the bar chart.
   a) Who is the youngest player to win a Grand Slam? How old was the player?
   b) Which players won a Grand Slam at age 16? Which tournaments did they win?
   c) Which Grand Slam did Pete Sampras win? How old was he?

2) The Australian Open is played in January.

JANUARY						
SUN	M	T	W	TH	F	SAT
				1	2	3
4	5	6	7	8	9	10
11	12	13	14	15	16	17
18	19	20	21	22	23	24
25	26	27	28	29	30	31

   a) If the tournament begins on the third Monday, what will the date be?
   b) The men's final will be held on January 31. What day of the week is this?

3) A box holds 24 tennis balls. If there are 9 boxes of balls, how many balls are there altogether?

4) A Wimbledon tennis ball weighs **2 ounces**. How much will 20 balls weigh?

5) If there are 20 balls on a court at any time and all the balls are changed every seven games, how many balls will be used for a 29-game match?

BLAST FROM THE PAST – THE MEN

Tennis, or lawn tennis, was invented in England in the late 1800s. Since then, there have been some great champions from all parts of the world.

BILL TILDEN

Bill Tilden was one of the first tennis players to be a strong athlete. He won his last doubles title in 1945 when he was 52 years old.

Date of birth: February 10, 1893
Nationality: American

Career wins/losses:
149 wins/19 losses

GRAND SLAMS – SINGLES
Wimbledon: 1920, 1921, 1930
US Open: 1920, 1921, 1922, 1923, 1924, 1925, 1929

Ranked Number 1: 1920, 1921, 1922, 1923, 1924, 1925, 1931

FRED PERRY

Fred Perry is the most successful British male player ever. He was a major celebrity in the UK as well as in the USA and Australia. He also helped launch a range of clothing that is still worn today.

Date of birth: May 18, 1909
Nationality: British

Career wins/losses:
140 wins/18 losses

GRAND SLAMS – SINGLES
Australian Open: 1934
French Open: 1935
Wimbledon: 1934, 1935, 1936
US Open: 1933, 1934, 1936

Ranked Number 1: 1934, 1935, 1936, 1937, 1941

KEN ROSEWALL

Ken Rosewall started playing tennis on his parents' court almost as soon as he could walk. He was a runner-up at Wimbledon four times but could never quite win it!

Date of birth: November 2, 1934
Nationality: Australian

Career wins/losses:
517 wins/165 losses

GRAND SLAMS – SINGLES
Australian Open: 1953, 1955, 1971, 1972
French Open: 1953, 1968
US Open: 1956, 1970

Ranked Number 1: 1960, 1961, 1962, 1963, 1964, 1970

BLAST FROM THE PAST MEN'S QUIZ

Answer these quiz questions about top players from days gone by.

1) Try these quick data collection questions.
   a) How old was Bill Tilden when he won Wimbledon the first time?
   b) How many singles Grand Slams did Ken Rosewall win?
   c) In which year did Fred Perry win three Grand Slams?

2) Look at the players' **Career wins/losses**. Give the total number of matches that each man played.

3) Put these years in order starting with the earliest.
   1909   1970   1956   1893   1929   1921   1964

4) Look at these sequences of years. Can you fill in the missing years?
   a) **1909   1918   ?   1936   1945   ?   1963**
   b) **1930   1933   1937   1942   ?   1955   ?**

5) Finally, try this fun activity. The tennis net has some shapes in it. What is the area of each shape? Give your answer in squares.

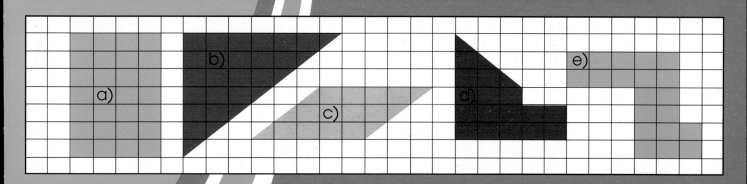

BLAST FROM THE PAST – THE WOMEN

There have been some great women tennis players in the history of the game.

CHARLOTTE COOPER

Charlotte Cooper won two Olympic tennis titles. She won the singles title and the mixed doubles at the Paris Olympics in 1900.

Date of birth:
September 22, 1870
Nationality: British

GRAND SLAMS – SINGLES
Wimbledon: 1895, 1896, 1898, 1901, 1908

HELEN WILLS MOODY

Helen Wills Moody was one of the first female players to be competitive and focus on winning every match. Until then, women's tennis had been about taking part, not winning.

Date of birth: October 6, 1905
Nationality: American

GRAND SLAMS – SINGLES
French Open: 1928, 1929, 1930, 1932
Wimbledon: 1927, 1928, 1929, 1930, 1932, 1933, 1935, 1938
US Open: 1923, 1924, 1925, 1927, 1928, 1929,1931

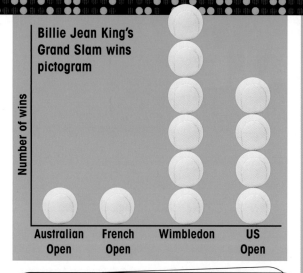

Number of wins

Australian Open | French Open | Wimbledon | US Open

BILLIE JEAN KING

Billie Jean King wins Wimbledon and lifts the "Rosewater Dish" in 1975.

In 1973, Billie played in a famous match known as the "Battle of the Sexes" against men's champion Bobby Riggs. Bobby claimed he could beat a top female player – but he couldn't beat Billie!

Date of birth: November 22, 1943
Nationality: American

GRAND SLAMS – SINGLES
Australian Open: 1968
French Open: 1972
Wimbledon: 1966, 1967, 1968, 1972, 1973, 1975
US Open: 1967, 1971, 1972, 1974

BLAST FROM THE PAST WOMEN'S QUIZ

Here are some quiz questions about top female players from history.

1) Try these quick data collection questions.
   a) How many US Opens did Helen Wills Moody win?
   b) Which Grand Slams did Billie Jean King win in 1972?
   c) How old was Charlotte Cooper when she won her last Wimbledon title? (Remember, the Wimbledon final takes place in July.)

2) Helen Wills Moody was ranked Number 1 female player in the world from 1927 to 1933 and then from 1935 to 1938. In how many years was she Number 1?

3) Look at this tally chart. Charlotte Cooper's Grand Slam wins have been filled in. Now draw the chart and fill in the tally marks for the other two players.

	Australian Open	French Open	Wimbledon	US Open
Charlotte Cooper			ⅢⅡ	
Helen Wills Moody				
Billie Jean King				

4) Look at the **Pictogram**. It shows Billie Jean King's Grand Slam wins. Draw a pictogram to show Helen Wills Moody's wins.

5) Look at Helen Wills Moody's Grand Slam wins. What is the ratio of Wimbledon wins to French Open wins?

GREATEST FEMALE PLAYERS

There are three female players who all qualify for the title of "The Greatest Female Player of All Time." Who do you think is best?

In 1988, Steffi Graf became the only player to win the "Golden Slam." This means she won four Grand Slams and an Olympic gold medal (shown here) in the same year!

Nationality: German
Career wins/losses singles:
900 wins/115 losses

GRAND SLAMS – SINGLES
Australian Open: 4
French Open: 6
Wimbledon: 7
US Open: 5

Ranked Number 1: 8 times

Margaret Court won more Grand Slam titles than any other player. She won 24 singles Grand Slams and 38 doubles Grand Slams.

Nationality: Australian
Career wins/losses singles:
1,177 wins/106 losses

GRAND SLAMS – SINGLES
Australian Open: 11
French Open: 5
Wimbledon: 3
US Open: 5

Ranked Number 1: 7 times

Nationality: American
Career wins/losses singles:
1,442 wins/219 losses

GRAND SLAMS – SINGLES
Australian Open: 3
French Open: 2
Wimbledon: 9
US Open: 4

Ranked Number 1: 7 times

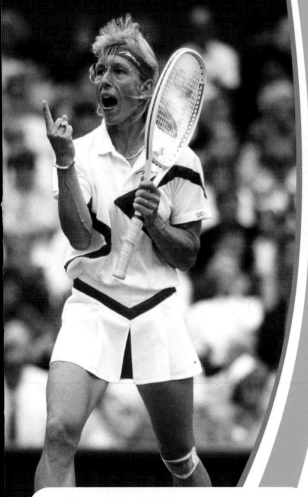

Martina Navratilova was a brilliant singles and doubles player. She won 177 doubles titles. Here, Martina celebrates being one point away from winning her ninth Wimbledon.

GREATEST FEMALE PLAYERS QUIZ

Now try these quiz questions.

1) This table shows the number of Grand Slam matches played by Martina Navratilova from 1973 to 2004.

Martina Navratilova		
GRAND SLAMS	Matches Won	Lost
Australian Open	46	7
French Open	51	11
Wimbledon	120	14
US Open	89	17

a) How many matches did Martina win?
b) How many matches did Martina play in total?

The table below shows the number of Grand Slam tournaments the three players entered. For example, Margaret won 11 of the 14 Australian Opens she entered.

Title Wins – Tournaments Entered			
	Margaret	Steffi	Martina
Australian Open	11–14	4–10	3–10
French Open	5–10	6–16	2–13
Wimbledon	3–12	7–15	9–23
US Open	5–11	5–15	4–21

2) Margaret won Wimbledon 3 times. She entered it 12 times. Write Margaret's wins as a fraction in its simplest form.

3) Margaret entered 10 French Open tournaments. What percentage did she win?

4) Write Steffi's US Open wins as a fraction in its simplest form.

5) Which tournament did Steffi win 40% of the time?

ROGER FEDERER – THE BEST EVER?

Many tennis fans believe Roger Federer is the best tennis player ever! He has won more Grand Slams than any other male player.

16

In January 2010, Roger won his 16th Grand Slam title at the Australian Open.

Australian Open: 4
French Open: 1
Wimbledon: 6
US Open: 5

6-1

Roger Federer is 6 ft 1 in tall.

81

Roger has won 81% of his singles matches. That's 81 out of every 100!

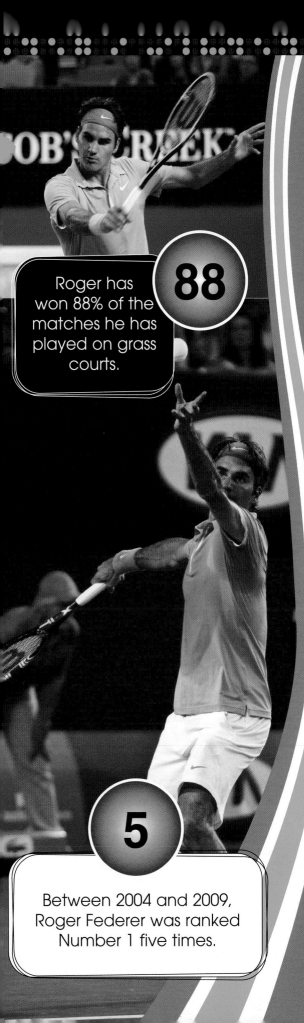

Roger has won 88% of the matches he has played on grass courts.

88

5

Between 2004 and 2009, Roger Federer was ranked Number 1 five times.

ROGER FEDERER QUIZ

Try these quiz questions about Roger Federer's amazing career.

1) Look at the numbers in the red circles.
   a) Which number is one quarter of 20?
   b) If I double this number, it is 176.
      If I subtract 65 from this number, the answer is 23. Which number is it?
   c) Round the numbers 16 and 81 to the nearest ten.

2) Write Roger's height in inches.
   Now write it in yards.

3) Look at Roger's Grand Slam wins.
   The numbers are **4**, **1**, **6**, and **5**. What is the highest number we can write using these digits? What is the lowest number?

4) In January 2010, Roger's career earnings reached **$50,777,919**. Can you write this large number in words?

5) Look at these tennis balls. Can you fill in the missing angles?

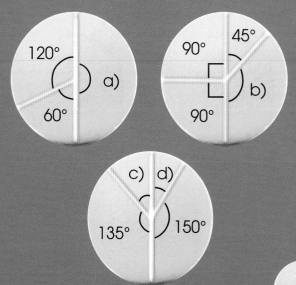

GREATEST MALE PLAYERS

There are three other male players who have earned the right to be at the top of the list of greatest all-time players.

PETE SAMPRAS
Date of birth: August 12, 1971
Nationality: American
Career wins/losses:
762 wins/222 losses
GRAND SLAMS – SINGLES
Australian Open: 2
Wimbledon: 7
US Open: 5
Ranked Number 1: 6 times

Pete started playing at the age of three when he found an old tennis racket in his house.

BJORN BORG
Date of birth: June 6, 1956
Nationality: Swedish
Career wins/losses:
597 wins/127 losses
GRAND SLAMS – SINGLES
French Open: 6
Wimbledon: 5
Ranked Number 1: 4 times

Bjorn Borg had great footwork and was brilliant at playing on the baseline. He shocked tennis fans by retiring when he was just 26 years old.

Baseline

ROD LAVER
Date of birth: August 9, 1938
Nationality: Australian
Career wins/losses:
392 wins/99 losses
GRAND SLAMS – SINGLES
Australian Open: 3
French Open: 2
Wimbledon: 4
US Open: 2
Ranked Number 1: 7 times

Rod Laver won all four Grand Slam tournaments in 1962. He then won all four again in 1969!

GREATEST MALE PLAYERS QUIZ

Now try these quiz questions.

1) Which of the three players has won the most singles Grand Slams? How many?

2) Write down each player's **Career wins/losses**. Now round each of the six numbers up or down to the nearest ten.

Now look at the **Grand Slams** table below.

GRAND SLAMS	Title Wins – Tournaments Entered		
	Rod	**Bjorn**	**Pete**
Australian Open	3–9	0–1	2–11
French Open	2–8	6–8	0–13
Wimbledon	4–11	5–9	7–14
US Open	2–12	0–9	5–14

It shows how many tournaments each player entered and won. For example, Rod won 3 of the 9 Australian Opens he entered. Rod's Australian Open wins can be shown as the fraction $1/3$. Rod won a third of the Australian Opens he entered.

3) Now write these players' wins as a fraction in its simplest form.
   a) Rod's US Open wins.
   b) Rod's French Open wins.
   c) Bjorn's French Open wins.
   d) Pete's Wimbledon wins.

4) Now show these results from the **Grand Slams** table as decimals.
   a) Rod's French Open wins.
   b) Pete's Wimbledon wins.

5) Which fraction in each pair is the larger?

   a) $1/2$ $2/5$ b) $3/4$ $7/8$ c) $3/5$ $1/3$

23

THE DAVIS CUP AND FED CUP

The Davis Cup is an annual competition held between men's tennis teams from around the world. The Fed Cup is an annual competition for women's teams. Each team is made up of the best players from that country.

Spain celebrates winning the 2009 Davis Cup.

The longest-ever Davis Cup singles match lasted 6 hours, 22 minutes. John McEnroe (USA) beat Mats Wilander (Sweden).

(Statistics up to end 2009)

DAVIS CUP RECORDS

Most matches won: 120
Nicola Pietrangeli, Italy

Youngest player:
Mohammed-Akhtar Hossain, Bangladesh, 13 years, 326 days

Oldest player:
Yaka-Garonfin Koptigan, Togo, 59 years, 147 days

(Statistics up to end 2009)

DAVIS CUP WINS

Team	Calculation		Wins
France	45 ÷ 5	=	?
Russia	–12 + 14	=	?
USA	4 x 8	=	?
Australia	56 ÷ 2	=	?
Germany	9 ÷ 3	=	?
Great Britain	20 – 11	=	?
Sweden	15 + 5 – 13	=	?
Spain	– 6 + 10	=	?

(Statistics up to end 2009)

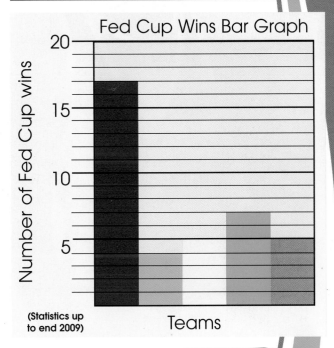

Fed Cup Wins Bar Graph

Number of Fed Cup wins

Teams

(Statistics up to end 2009)

FED CUP RECORDS

Most matches won: 72
Arantxa Sánchez Vicario,
Spain

Youngest player:
Denise Panagopoulou,
Greece, 12 years, 360 days

Oldest player:
Gill Butterfield,
Bermuda, 52 years, 162 days

(Statistics up to end 2009)

TEAM TENNIS QUIZ

Answer these quiz questions about the Davis Cup and Fed Cup.

1) Look at the **Davis Cup Wins** table. Make each of the calculations to find out how many times each team has won the competition.

2) Now make a list showing the teams and their results in order with the highest number of wins at the top.

3) Write down all the factors of 32.

4) Look at the **Fed Cup Wins Bar Graph**. Use these statements to match the colors of the bars to the five teams.
   - The USA has won the most Fed Cups.
   - Czechoslovakia won the same number of Fed Cups as Spain.
   - Australia won three more Fed Cups than Russia.
   How many times has each team won the Fed Cup?

5) A ticket to see a Fed Cup match costs $36.00.
   a) How much will it cost to buy four tickets?
   b) If you buy one ticket, a sandwich for $3.60, and a bottle of water for $2.00, how much change will you get from $48.00?

THE WILLIAMS SISTERS

American tennis champions Serena and Venus Williams are sisters first and tennis rivals second. They grew up playing tennis and were coached by their father, Richard Williams.

Venus (left) and Serena in 1999.

Venus won the Olympic singles gold medal in 2000. Venus and Serena won the Olympic doubles gold medals in 2000 and 2008.

WILLIAMS SISTERS WIN – LOSS TABLE

This table shows each sister's number of wins and losses each year.
For example, in 2000, Serena won 37 matches and lost eight matches.

	2000	2001	2002	2003	2004	2005	2006	2007	2008	2009
Serena	37–8	38–7	56–5	38–3	39–9	21–7	12–4	35–10	44–8	50–12
Venus	41–4	46–5	62–9	26–5	44–12	37–10	13–6	50–10	40–11	38–16

SERENA

Height: 5 ft 9 in

GRAND SLAMS – SINGLES
Australian Open: 2003, 2005, 2007, 2009, 2010
French Open: 2002
Wimbledon: 2002, 2003, 2009, 2010
US Open: 1999, 2002, 2008

VENUS

Height: 6 ft 1 in

GRAND SLAMS – SINGLES
Wimbledon: 2000, 2001, 2005, 2007, 2008
US Open: 2000, 2001

CHAMPION SISTERS QUIZ

Try these Williams sisters quiz questions.

1) Look at the **Williams Sisters Win/Loss Table**.
   a) Which year did Serena play 48 matches?
   b) In which year did Venus play 31 matches?
   c) Who won more matches in 2007?
   d) Who played more matches in 2008?

2) Serena won 21 out of 28 matches in 2005. What percentage is this?

3) Between 2000 and 2009, which sister played more matches? How many more? Which sister won more matches? How many more?

4) Look at the six measurements below.
   a) Which is closer to Serena's height?
   b) Which is closer to Venus's height?

   2 yd   79 in   1.9 yd   70 in   2.1 yd   81 in

5) These analog and digital clocks show some competition start times. Can you match the analog clocks to the digital clocks that show the same time?

NADAL VS MURRAY

Rafael Nadal and Andy Murray are two of the best male players around. They often clash in the final of important tournaments. Nadal and Murray were born less than a year apart, but Nadal rose to the top quicker.

Andy Murray is the number one British tennis player.

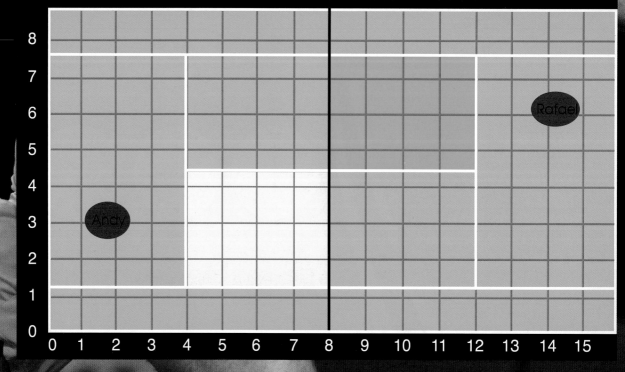

IN OR OUT? GRID MAP

RIVALS QUIZ

Now try these quiz questions about Nadal and Murray.

1) This table shows how many matches Rafael won and lost each year. Work out Andy's win/loss numbers using these statements.

	RAFAEL Win/Loss	ANDY Win/Loss
2005	79–10	
2006	59–12	
2007	70–15	
2008	82–11	
2009	64–14	

- **2005 – Andy won 14 out of 24 matches.**
- **2006 – Andy lost 25 matches out of 65.**
- **2007 – Andy won 43 matches out of 57.**
- **2008 – Andy won 56 out of 71 matches.**
- **2009 – Andy lost 11 matches out of 77.**

2) Look at Rafael's number of wins over the five years. Use a calculator to find the mean.

3) Now work out the mean of Andy's wins. Whose mean is higher?

Look at the **In or Out? Grid Map**. Andy and Rafael are serving to each other. To be "in," Andy's serve must land in the blue area. Rafael's serve must land in the yellow area.

4) Rafael serves first. If the ball lands on these grid coordinates will it be in or out?
a) **(6,3)**   b) **(7,4)**   c) **(3,1)**   d) **(2,4)**

5) Andy serves to these coordinates. Are Andy's serves in or out?
a) **(13,7)**   b) **(10,6)**
c) **(9,5)**   d) **(13,8)**

Rafael Nadal won the French Open four times in a row in 2005, 2006, 2007, and 2008! He also won Wimbledon and an Olympic singles gold medal in 2008.

9 RECORD BREAKERS QUIZ

1 665 minutes
2 3 hours and 35 minutes
3 Federer and
Sampras $7.5 million
Agassi $19.7 million
Nadal $25.6 million
Becker $25.7 million
4 2 minutes
5 Answers will vary.

11 SCORING QUIZ

1 Score B
Murray 2 Federer 1
Score C
Murray 3 Federer 2
2 Murray
3 18 games; sets 2 and 3
4 Yes
5 18 games

13 GRAND SLAM QUIZ

1 a) Lottie Dod; 15 years old
b) Tracy Austin, US Open;
Martina Hingis, Australian
Open; Monica Seles,
French Open
c) US Open; 19 years old
2 a) January 19 b) Saturday
3 216
4 40 ounces or 2.5 pounds
5 100 balls

15 BLAST FROM THE PAST MEN'S QUIZ

1 a) 27 b) 8 c) 1934
2 Bill Tilden 168
Fred Perry 158
Ken Rosewall 682
3 1893 1909 1921 1929
1956 1964 1970
4 a) 1927, 1954
b) 1948, 1963
5 a) 28 squares b) 24.5
squares c) 15 squares

d) 17.5 squares
e) 20 squares

17 BLAST FROM THE PAST WOMEN'S QUIZ

1 a) 7   b) French Open,
Wimbledon, US Open
c) 37
2 11 years
3 Your tally chart should look
like this.

	Australian Open	French Open	Wimbledon	US Open
Charlotte Cooper			ЖНТ	
Helen Wills Moody		IIII	ЖНТ III	ЖНТ II
Billie Jean King	I	I	ЖНТ I	IIII

4 Helen Wills Moody's
pictogram will look like this.

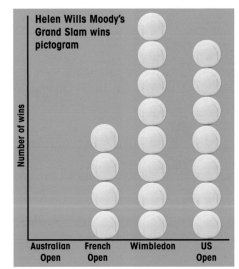

Helen Wills Moody's Grand Slam wins pictogram

5 2:1

19 GREATEST FEMALE PLAYERS QUIZ

1 a) 306   b) 355
2 $^1/_4$ 3 50% 4 $^1/_3$
5 Australian Open

21 ROGER FEDERER QUIZ

1 a) 5 b) 88 c) 20; 80
2 73 in; 2.08 yd
3 Highest 6,541; lowest 1,456
4 Fifty million, seven hundred
seventy-seven thousand,
nine hundred nineteen
dollars

5 a) 180° b) 135° c) 45° d) 30°

23 GREATEST MALE PLAYERS QUIZ

1 Pete Sampras; 14
2 760 220 600 130 390 100
3 a) $^1/_6$ b) $^1/_4$
c) $^3/_4$ d) $^1/_2$
4 a) 0.25 b) 0.5
5 a) $^1/_2$ b) $^7/_8$ c) $^3/_5$

25 TEAM TENNIS QUIZ

1 France 9; Russia 2; USA 32;
Australia 28; Germany 3;
Great Britain 9; Sweden 7;
Spain 4
2 USA 32
Australia 28
France/Great Britain 9
Sweden 7
Spain 4
Germany 3
Russia 2
3 1, 2, 4, 8, 16, 32
4 USA red 17; Czechoslovakia
and Spain orange/yellow 5;
Russia green 4; Australia
blue 7
5 a) $144.00   b) $6.40

27 CHAMPION SISTERS QUIZ

1 a) 2004 b) 2003 c) Venus
d) Serena
2 75%
3 Venus played 42 more;
Venus won 27 more
4 a) 70 in
b) 2 yd
5 a/g b/h c/e d/f

29 RIVALS QUIZ

1 2005 14–10; 2006 40–25;
2007 43–14; 2008 56–15;
2009 66–11
2 70.8 3 43.8; Rafael's
4 a) In b) In c) Out d) Out
5 a) Out b) In c) In d) Out

ace: a point scored when a player hits a serve that the opponent can't return

advantage: the name for the first point scored after the score in a game reaches 40–40

baseline: one of the boundary lines at each end of the tennis court

consecutive: following one after the other

coordinate: any of a set of numbers used to tell the location of a point on a grid

data: facts or statistics

doubles: a match with two people on each side

footwork: use of the feet in changing direction and position

Grand Slam: the name for one of the four biggest tennis tournaments: Wimbledon, US Open, French Open, Australian Open

grid: a network of evenly spaced lines running across and up and down

match: a series of sets played until one side wins two out of three or three out of five sets

mixed doubles: a doubles match in which men and women compete together

runner-up: the person who finishes second in a competition

serve: to hit the ball to begin play

service box: the area in which a player stands to serve

set: a series of games played until one side wins at least six games and beats the opponent by at least two games, or wins a tiebreaker

singles: a match with one person on each side

statistics: a collection of facts in the form of numbers

tiebreaker: the 13th game in a set, played to break a tie of 6–6

tournament: a series of matches that make up a single competition

ace 6

angles 21

Australian Open 7, 12–15, 17, 18–20, 22, 23, 27

Borg, Bjorn 22, 23

Cooper, Charlotte 16, 17

coordinates 29

Court, Margaret 18, 19

data 15, 17

decimals 23

doubles 7, 10, 14, 18, 19, 26

factors 25

Federer, Roger 8, 11, 20, 21

fraction 19, 23

French Open 7, 8, 12–20, 22, 23, 27

games 6, 8, 9, 11, 13

Graf, Steffi 9, 18, 19

Grand Slams 7, 8, 12–23, 27

grid map 28, 29

King, Billie Jean 17

Laver, Rod 23

matches 6, 8, 9, 11, 13, 15, 19, 20, 21, 24–27, 29

mean (average) 9, 29

mixed doubles 16

Moody, Helen Wills 16, 17

Murray, Andy 28, 29

Nadal, Rafael 8, 12, 28, 29

Navratilova, Martina 9, 19

Olympics 16, 18, 26

percentage 19, 27

Perry, Fred 14, 15

Roddick, Andy 8, 11

Rosewall, Ken 15

rounding 21, 23

Sampras, Pete 8, 22, 23

scoring 11

sequences 15

serve 6, 8, 29

sets 6, 11

singles 10, 14–20, 22, 23, 26

statistics 8, 24, 25

surfaces 7

Tilden, Bill 14, 15

tournament 12, 13, 19, 23, 28

US Open 7, 12–20, 22, 23, 27

Williams sisters 6, 7, 26, 27

Wimbledon 7, 8, 12–20, 22, 23, 27